NETHERLANDS

EXPLORE THE COUNTRIES

Big Buddy Books
An Imprint of Abdo Publishing
abdopublishing.com

Julie Murray

abdopublishing.com

Published by Abdo Publishing, a division of ABDO, PO Box 398166, Minneapolis, Minnesota 55439.
Copyright © 2018 by Abdo Consulting Group, Inc. International copyrights reserved in all countries. No part
of this book may be reproduced in any form without written permission from the publisher. Big Buddy Books™
is a trademark and logo of Abdo Publishing.

Printed in the United States of America, North Mankato, Minnesota.
052017
092017

Cover Photo: ©iStockphoto.com.
Interior Photos: American Photo Archive/Alamy Stock Photo (p. 15); David R. Frazier Photolibrary, Inc./Alamy
    Stock Photo (p. 34); dpa picture alliance/Alamy Stock Photo (pp. 19, 29); FineArt/Alamy Stock Photo
    (p. 31); Roberto Fumagalli/Alamy Stock Photo (p. 35); GL Archive/Alamy Stock Photo (p. 31); Granger,
    NYC — All rights reserved (pp. 13, 16); ©iStockphoto.com (pp. 5, 9, 11, 17, 23, 27, 34, 35, 37, 38);
    ton koene/Alamy Stock Photo (p. 23); Jason Langley/Alamy Stock Photo (p. 25); frans lemmens/Alamy
    Stock Photo (p. 19); Henk Meijer/Alamy Stock Photo (p. 21); Shutterstock.com (pp. 11, 35); ullstein bild/
    Granger, NYC — All rights reserved (p. 33); United Archives GmbH/Alamy Stock Photo (p. 33).

Coordinating Series Editor: Tamara L. Britton
Editor: Katie Lajiness
Graphic Design: Taylor Higgins, Keely McKernan

Country population and area figures taken from the CIA World Factbook.

Publisher's Cataloging-in-Publication Data

Names: Murray, Julie, 1969- , author.
Title: Netherlands / by Julie Murray.
Description: Minneapolis, MN : Abdo Publishing, 2018. | Series: Explore the
    countries | Includes bibliographical references and index.
Identifiers: LCCN 2016962351 | ISBN 9781532110504 (lib. bdg.) |
    ISBN 9781680788358 (ebook)
Subjects: LCSH: Netherlands--Juvenile literature.
Classification: DDC 949.2--dc23
LC record available at http://lccn.loc.gov/2016962351

NETHERLANDS

CONTENTS

Around the World

Our world has many countries. Each country has beautiful land. It has its own rich history. And, the people have their own languages and ways of life.

The Netherlands is a country in Europe. What do you know about the Netherlands? Let's learn more about this place and its story!

 Did You Know?

Dutch is the official language of the Netherlands.

In the Netherlands, there are more bicycles than people. The country is one of the most bike-friendly places in the world.

Passport to The Netherlands

The Netherlands is a small country in northwestern Europe. It shares borders with Germany to the east and Belgium to the south. The North Sea is to the north and west.

The country's total area is about 16,040 square miles (41,543 sq km). More than 17 million people live there.

WHERE IN THE WORLD?

North Sea

NETHERLANDS

GERMANY

BELGIUM

Did You Know?

Netherlands is almost twice the size of New Jersey.

IMPORTANT CITIES

Amsterdam is the **capital** and largest city in the Netherlands. More than 1 million people live there. This city is the country's **economic** center. It is also a popular place to visit.

The city has been an important port for hundreds of years. In the 1200s, the city began as a fishing village. Today, boats still travel along Amsterdam's **canals**. More than 1,000 bridges allow people to pass over the water.

SAY IT
Amsterdam
AM-stuhr-dam

The Python Bridge was built in 2001. It is for pedestrians and bicyclists.

There are three I amsterdam sculptures throughout Amsterdam. One sculpture is often moved to different places around the city.

Rotterdam is the second-largest city in the Netherlands. Almost 1 million people live there. Shipping is the city's largest business. Other major businesses include oil and gas.

The Hague is the third-largest city. About 650,000 people call it home. The Dutch government meets in The Hague.

Did You Know?

The people of the Netherlands are called the Dutch.

SAY IT

Rotterdam
RAH-tuhr-dam

The Hague
THUH HAYG

The Oude Haven is the oldest harbor in Rotterdam. It was built in the 1300s.

The Het Binnenhof in The Hague has been a meeting place for the government since 1446.

The Netherlands in History

More than 2,000 years ago, the Roman Empire took over what is now the Netherlands, Belgium, and Luxembourg. By the 1400s, a royal family controlled the area.

In the 1600s, the Dutch set up **colonies** around the world. During this time, they fought many wars with England.

For hundreds of years, the Dutch were under Spanish control. Then, they spent much of the 1700s fighting the French.

In 1673, the Dutch fought the British and the French in the Battle of Texel.

13

After centuries of battles, the Dutch decided not to fight anymore. So, the country did not choose sides during **World War I** and **World War II**.

However, Germany took over the Netherlands in 1940. They sent **Jewish** people to **concentration camps**. Sadly, many died before the war ended.

After the war, the Netherlands set its remaining **colonies** free. Many people from these colonies then moved to the Netherlands.

In 1945, the Canadian Army helped free the Netherlands from German control.

BEVEROL
AUTO-MOTOR-OLIE

15

TIMELINE

1624

The Dutch West India Company created **colonies** in the United States. They controlled parts of what is now New York, New Jersey, Connecticut, and Delaware.

1899

The Hague held its first peace conference. Leaders from 26 countries met there.

1810

Napoleon claimed the Netherlands for France. Three years later, the Dutch drove out the French.

1940

German troops took
control of the country.

2002

The Netherlands began using
the euro as its currency.

2013

Queen Beatrix stepped
down at the age of 75.

AN IMPORTANT SYMBOL

The Dutch flag was adopted in 1937. It has three stripes. They are red, white, and blue.

The government is a **constitutional monarchy**. The country's prime minister runs the government. The king and queen have less power.

The Netherlands is divided into 12 provinces. This is a large section within a country, like a state.

In 2010, Mark Rutte became prime minister.

In 1789, the Dutch were the first country to use red, white, and blue in the flag.

Willem-Alexander became king in 2013.

SAY IT

Mark Rutte
MAHRK ROOT-ah

Willem-Alexander
WIH-luhm ah-lehk-SAHN-duhr

ACROSS THE LAND

In the Netherlands, winters are warm and summers are cool. The weather is often chilly and rainy. On average, there are only about 25 clear days each year.

The country has flat, low land. The lowest point in the Netherlands is about 22 feet (7 m) below sea level. The country's highest point is Vaalserberg, a hill in the mainland. It stands 1,056 feet (322 m) high.

Did You Know?

In January, the Netherland's average temperature is 35°F (2°C). In July, it is 63°F (17°C).

A network of pumps and canals keeps the sea from flooding the land. Windmills used to pump the water. Today, electric pumps do the work.

The Netherlands is home to many plants and trees. Forests cover about 10 percent of the country. The Scots pine is the most common tree.

Sea birds live along the country's coast. Badgers, deer, fox, mice, and muskrats are common throughout the country.

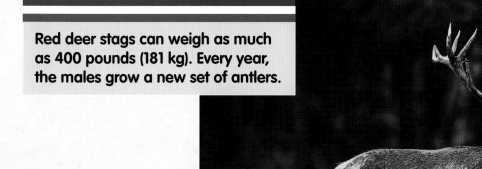

Red deer stags can weigh as much as 400 pounds (181 kg). Every year, the males grow a new set of antlers.

Seagulls hunt for fish along the coast of the Netherlands.

Earning a Living

The Netherlands has a strong **economy**. Major businesses include banking, energy, and health care. Factories make food products, machinery, metals, and oil products.

Some people are farmers. Farmers raise cattle, pigs, chickens, and sheep. Common crops include grains, potatoes, and sugar beets.

The Netherlands is home to large natural gas fields. Natural gas comes from the ground. The province of Groningen has the country's largest reserves.

50 TULPEN 7.00

25

LIFE IN THE NETHERLANDS

The Netherlands has a rich **culture** with great art and food. There are many museums throughout the country. Dutch painters, such as Rembrandt van Rijn and Johannes Vermeer, are known throughout the world.

Dutch foods are very rich. People in the Netherlands eat a lot of hard cheeses, pancakes, and pastries. Foods from Indonesia are also very popular.

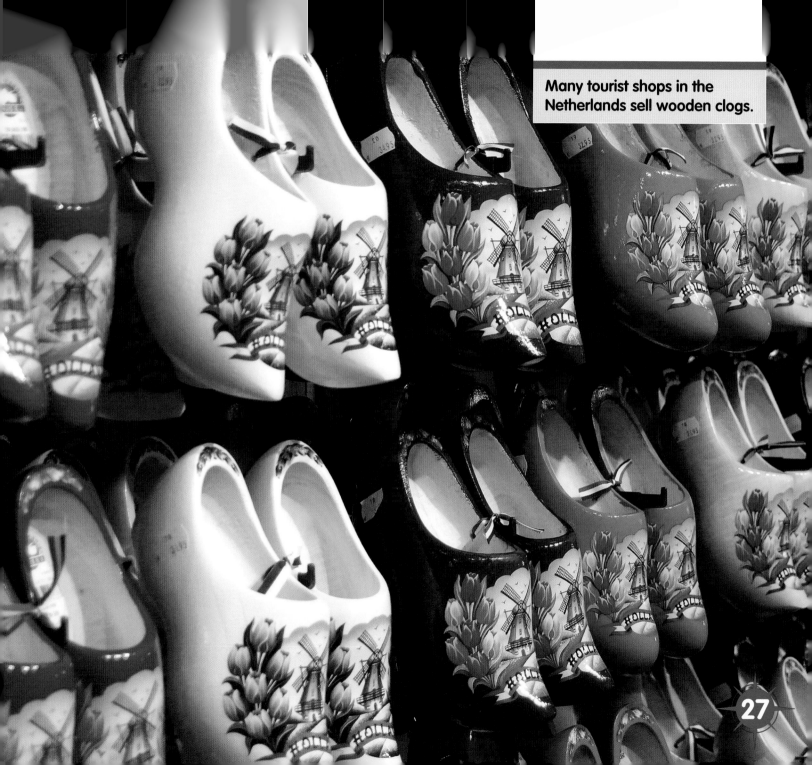

Many tourist shops in the Netherlands sell wooden clogs.

People in the Netherlands enjoy watching and playing sports such as tennis and ice skating. More than half of all Dutch ride their bikes every day. They ride for sport, to travel, or just for fun.

There are different faiths in the Netherlands. About half of Dutch people are **Christians**. However, many people in the Netherlands do not follow a religion.

Did You Know?

In the Netherlands, students must attend school from ages 5 to 16. Most people attend school until they are 18.

Anna van der Breggen is a Dutch cyclist. She won a gold medal in the 2016 Olympics in Rio de Janeiro, Brazil.

Famous Faces

   Many talented people have lived in the Netherlands. Vincent van Gogh was born on March 30, 1853, in Zundert, Netherlands. He is considered to be one of the greatest painters in history.

   Van Gogh sold few paintings during his lifetime. His paintings became famous after his death in 1890. A hundred years later, van Gogh's paintings became very popular. In 2015, one of his paintings sold for more than $66 million.

Throughout his career, van Gogh painted 36 pictures of himself.

Van Gogh is known for his use of color and his brushwork.

Anne Frank was born on June 12, 1929, in Frankfurt, Germany. During **World War II**, Frank's family and four other **Jewish** people went into hiding in Amsterdam. She kept a diary while they lived in the back room of a business.

In 1944, the family was sent to a **concentration camp** in Germany. The next year, Frank died in the camp. Her father was the only family member to survive the war. Two years later, Frank's diary became a book for the world to read.

Frank started writing in her diary on her 13th birthday. She wrote about her thoughts and feelings, as well as short stories.

Frank's diary has been printed in 70 languages and in more than 60 countries.

TOUR BOOK

Imagine traveling to the Netherlands! Here are some places you could go and things you could do.

Remember

The Anne Frank House is a museum. See the hidden area where she and seven others spent two years during **World War II**.

See

The windmills of Schiedam are the largest in the world. Some are up to 108 feet (33 m) tall.

 # Explore

The Keukenhof is a park featuring more than 7 million flower bulbs in bloom. See and smell more than 800 kinds of tulips.

Discover

The Artis Royal Zoo was founded in 1838. There are more than 700 kinds of animals from around the world.

 # Travel

The Emperor's **Canal** is one of three main canals in Amsterdam. Dug in 1612, it is the widest canal in the city.

A Great Country

The story of the Netherlands is important to our world. The Netherlands is a land of windmills and tulips. It is a country of strong people.

The people and places that make up Netherlands offer something special. They help make the world a more beautiful, interesting place.

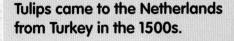

Tulips came to the Netherlands from Turkey in the 1500s.

Netherlands Up Close

Official Name: Kingdom of the Netherlands

Flag:

Population (rank): 17,016,967
(July 2016 est.)
(67th most-populated country)

Total Area (rank): 16,040 square miles
(135th largest country)

Capital: Amsterdam

Official Language: Dutch

Currency: Euro

Form of Government: Constitutional monarchy

National Anthem: "Het Wilhelmus" ("The William")

IMPORTANT WORDS

canal an artificial waterway for boats.

capital often a city where government leaders meet. In the Netherlands, the government meets in The Hague.

Christian (KHRIS-chuhn) a person who practices Christianity, which is a religion that follows the teaching of Jesus Christ.

colony land settled by people from another area.

concentration camp a place where persons (as prisoners of war, political prisoners, or refugees) are held.

constitutional monarchy (kahnt-stuh-TOO-shnuhl MAH-nuhr-kee) a form of government in which a king or queen has only those powers given by a country's laws and constitution.

culture (KUHL-chuhr) the arts, beliefs, and ways of life of a group of people.

economy the way that a country produces, sells, and buys goods and services.

Jewish a person who practices Judaism, which is a religion based on laws recorded in the Torah, or is related to the ancient Hebrews.

World War I a war fought in Europe from 1914 to 1918.

World War II a war fought in Europe, Asia, and Africa from 1939 to 1945.

WEBSITES

To learn more about Explore the Countries, visit **abdobooklinks.com**. These links are routinely monitored and updated to provide the most current information available.

INDEX